DEC 0 3 2012

TOP 25

FOOTBALL SKILLS, TIPS, AND TRICKS

Enslow Publishers, Inc.
40 Industrial Road
Box 398
Berkeley Heights, NJ 07922
USA

http://www.enslow.com

JOHN ALBERT TORRES

Library of Congress Cataloging-in-Publication Data

Torres, John Albert.
  Top 25 football skills, tips, and tricks / John Albert Torres.
      p. cm. — (Top 25 sports skills, tips, and tricks)
  Includes index.
  Summary: "Discusses football skills, including the proper techniques for passing, rushing, receiving, blocking, and tackling and provides tips for offense, defense, and special teams, including drills and tricks from the pros"—Provided by publisher.
  ISBN 978-0-7660-3858-5
  1. Football—Training—Juvenile literature. I. Title.
  GV953.5.T67 2012
  796.332—dc22

                          2011005925

Paperback ISBN 978-1-59845-355-3

Printed in the United States of America

052011 Lake Book Manufacturing, Inc., Melrose Park, IL

10 9 8 7 6 5 4 3 2 1

Do not attempt the more advanced skills and tricks without adult supervision.

To Our Readers:
We have done our best to make sure all Internet addresses in this book were active and appropriate when we went to press. However, the author and the publisher have no control over and assume no liability for the material available on those Internet sites or on other Web sites they may link to. Any comments or suggestions can be sent by e-mail to comments@enslow.com or to the address on the back cover.

♻ Enslow Publishers, Inc., is committed to printing our books on recycled paper. The paper in every book contains 10% to 30% post-consumer waste (PCW). The cover board on the outside of each book contains 100% PCW. Our goal is to do our part to help young people and the environment too!

Illustration Credits: AP Images, p. 21; AP Images / AJ Mast, p. 39; AP Images / Bill Baptist, p. 11; AP Images / Brian Garfinkel, p. 17; AP Images / Chuck Burton, p. 31; AP Images / Darron Cummings, p. 19; AP Images / David Drapkin, pp. 9, 27; AP Images / David Stluka, p. 25; AP Images / Michael Conroy, p. 7; AP Images / Nam Y. Huh, p. 32; AP Images / Paul Jasienski, p. 35; AP Images / Paul Spinelli, pp. 29, 43; AP Images / Ted S. Warren, p. 41; Enslow Publishers, Inc., p. 4; Ken Argent / Frozen Image Photography, pp. 1, 5, 10, 13, 14, 18, 20, 28, 33, 37; Shutterstock.com, pp. 6, 12, 15, 22, 23, 24, 38, 44, 45.

Cover Illustration: Ken Argent / Frozen Image Photography (Young player running with the football).

CONTENTS

★**Passing and Receiving 5**

1. Gripping the Football, 6
2. The Proper Throwing Stance, 8
3. How to Fling the Pigskin, 10
4. Catching the Football, 11
5. Running After the Catch, 12

★**Rushing 14**

6. The Exchange, 15
7. Protecting the Ball, 16
8. Running to "Daylight," 18
9. Running Vision, 20
10. More Than Just a Runner, 21

★**Line Play 22**

11. Run Blocking, 23
12. Blocking for the Trap, 24
13. Pass Blocking, 26
14. Defensive Line, 28
15. Patience on Defense, 29

★**Defense and Special Teams 30**

16. How to Tackle, 30
17. Linebackers, 32
18. Pass Coverage, 34
19. Punting and Special Teams Coverage, 36
20. Kicking Field Goals, 38

★**Fun Tricks and Training 40**

21. Agility Drills, 40
22. Conditioning, 42
23. Terrible 20s, 43
24. Two-Hand Touch, 44
25. Fun Plays, 45

Glossary, 46
Further Reading (Books and Internet Addresses), 47
Index, 48

10 YDS **GOALPOST**

END ZONE

1 YD **5 YDS**

160 FT

100 YDS

RB   RB
QB
WR TE T G C G T   WR
DE DT DT DE
CB LB   LB CB
LB
S   S

END ZONE

GOALPOST **10 YDS**

TEAM BENCH

TEAM BENCH

OFFENSE
Q–Quarterback
RB–Running Back
WR–Wide Receiver
TE–Tight End
C–Center
G–Guard
T–Tackle

DEFENSE
DT–Defensive Tackle
DE–Defensive End
LB–Linebacker
S–Safety
CB–Cornerback

4

PASSING AND RECEIVING

There are many exciting plays in football. There is the last-second field goal, the interception return for a touchdown, long punt returns, and the running back that outraces everybody else on his way to the end zone.

But perhaps no play during a football game causes everyone to stand up and cheer like watching the quarterback complete a long pass downfield to a speedy wide receiver.

Many things have to occur in order to complete a successful pass play, even a short pass. First, the offensive line must block. Then the quarterback has to spot an open receiver. Next, the quarterback has to deliver a good pass. Finally, the receiver—whether it is a running back, tight end, or wide receiver—has to catch the pass.

A long touchdown pass can be one of the most exciting plays in football. But a successful pass play requires more than just a perfect pass from the quarterback. All eleven players on offense must do their job well to complete a pass.

GRIPPING THE FOOTBALL

You have to know how to properly grip a football before you can throw it. The right way for the quarterback to hold a football is by mainly using your fingers. Do not cradle the ball in the palm of your hand. Hand size is also important. If you have small hands, move your hand to the back half of the ball. Average or large-sized hands can hold the ball closer to the center. Run your fingers across the laces and keep your index finger behind the laces, toward the top of the ball. Now you are ready to start throwing. Many coaches tell their quarterbacks to train with a heavier ball, about two pounds, in order to help increase finger and hand strength.

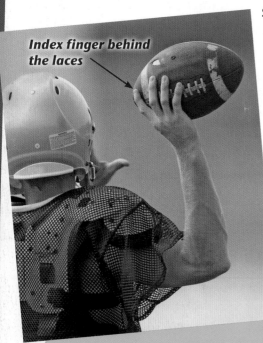

Index finger behind the laces

The proper grip of a football is essential to a good throw.

Pro Tips and Tricks

Former Indianapolis Colts head coach Tony Dungy said All-Pro quarterback Peyton Manning is the best when it comes to getting ready for a game. "The thing that separates Peyton is his preparation. He never goes into a game when he's not fully prepared. He believes if you're prepared and you know what to do, you're going to have a high chance of success."

Indianapolis Colts All-Pro quarterback Peyton Manning is one of the best in the National Football League (NFL). Manning can deliver passes with pinpoint accuracy, but he has to do more than just throw a perfect spiral. The quarterback must run the offense, which includes calling the plays and reading the defense before the ball is snapped.

Footwork is important for a quarterback. For a right-handed player, your first step from center should be straight back with your right foot, then crossover with your left. You don't want to trip over your linemen!

2 THE PROPER THROWING STANCE

The proper stance is in many ways as important for a quarterback as the grip. After you receive the ball from the center, start moving back with both hands on the ball. As you drop back, keep your head up. You drop back from the line of scrimmage to keep space between you and your blockers. Look for receivers trying to get open. But also watch out for defensive players hoping to sack you.

When you're ready to throw, your non-throwing foot (for a right-handed quarterback, this would be your left foot) should be forward. Point this foot toward your intended target, with your shoulders nearly parallel to the target as well. Take your non-throwing hand off the ball and hold it about as high as the bottom of your facemask. Then, start bringing your throwing arm back to make your toss.

Did You Know?

Hall of Fame football legend George Blanda, who died in 2010, was one of the best quarterbacks of his generation. He starred for the Chicago Bears, Houston Oilers, and Oakland Raiders. But he was actually even better at kicking. He holds the all-time record for most extra points kicked.

Scan the field with your eyes; do not stare at the receiver you want to throw the ball to until you're ready to throw.

Pull your arm back when ready to throw.

New England Patriots quarterback Tom Brady displays the proper throwing form. A two-time NFL MVP, Brady set a single-season record for touchdown passes with fifty in 2007.

Point your non-throwing foot forward, aimed at your target.

3 HOW TO FLING THE PIGSKIN

Throwing a football is much different than throwing a baseball or basketball. The ball's shape makes throwing it unique. Bend your throwing elbow and cock your arm. Your body should not be perfectly balanced. Instead, the bulk of your weight should be on your back foot. When you are ready to throw, step forward and transfer your weight forward while letting the ball slide off your fingers into a tight spiral. Make sure the ball comes off your index finger and that you follow through properly. This is like a baseball pitcher making sure that his arm continues moving forward even after the ball is released.

Release the ball off your index finger and follow through.

Bend throwing elbow

Transfer your weight forward from your back foot to your front foot as you throw.

Throwing a football accurately is not easy. It takes a lot of practice. Repeating the correct motion over and over will help you make more consistent and accurate passes.

 CATCHING THE FOOTBALL

The ball is in the air. As a receiver hoping to catch the ball, what should you do? First, you need to run the proper pass pattern. This means you run to a certain spot on the field. The receivers run different patterns, or routes. It is important to practice running the proper route. The quarterback will expect you to be there, and he will throw it to that spot.

Most young players want to catch the ball in their chests. But the proper way is to catch it with both hands. Form a triangle with your thumbs and index fingers. Once you catch it, pull the ball close to your body. Practice by tossing yourself the football. Try to catch it with your fingers around the fat part of the ball. Now, turn your body and start racing for the end zone.

Watch the ball all the way into your hands.

Form a triangle with your thumbs and index fingers.

Houston Texans All-Pro Andre Johnson has the prototype build for a wide receiver: big, strong, and fast. But most important, he has great hands. A receiver with great hands will gain the trust of his quarterback, and he will see a lot more balls thrown his way.

RUNNING AFTER THE CATCH

Once you catch the ball and begin running, you must expect to be hit hard and often. The number one priority after catching a pass is to protect the football. A defensive player would like nothing more than to knock the ball loose. A fun way to practice protecting the football is to spend some time during the day holding a football. Tell your family and friends to occasionally knock the ball out of your hands. Squeezing the ball during the day will also help make your fingers stronger.

Wide receivers can expect contact at the line of scrimmage from defensive backs. You must break free from them to run the proper pass route. Once you catch the ball, secure it, keep your head up, and run forward to the end zone.

THEN AND NOW

The tight end position has changed drastically over the years. From the 1950s through the 1970s, tight ends were rarely used for catching passes. Instead, their main function was to block as an additional offensive lineman. Now most teams use the tight end as a receiver and a blocker.

The quarterback won't make a perfect throw every time. Be ready to dive for a low pass or jump in the air for a high pass. Be ready for a hit from a defender. Concentrate and you might come down with an acrobatic catch!

RUSHING

Every football coach will tell you the same thing: If you don't rush the football successfully then you will not win the game. Even if you have a great passing attack, a good running game—or rushing attack—will allow you to control the tempo of the game.

Rushing the ball also helps the passing attack because the defenders will not know what kind of play to expect. Without a running game, the opposing defense can drop extra players into coverage to stop the pass.

Like a successful passing play, a good run relies on many things to happen correctly. First, the ball has to be hiked properly from the center to the quarterback. Then the handoff exchange between the quarterback and running back has to be smooth. Next, the offensive line needs to create holes for the running back to rush through. Lastly, the running back needs to have the vision to find the running lanes and explode through them.

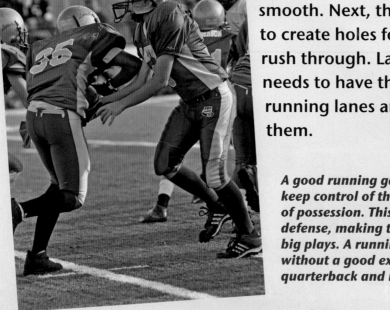

A good running game will help an offense keep control of the ball and maintain time of possession. This will tire out the opposing defense, making them more vulnerable to big plays. A running game cannot begin without a good exchange between the quarterback and running back.

 # THE EXCHANGE

Perhaps the thing youth football coaches practice the most is the exchange, or handoff, between quarterback and running back. It sounds simple enough, but the exchange needs to be smooth. Getting a good exchange prevents fumbles, which can give the ball to the other team. Much like the way a baseball catcher creates a target for his pitcher to throw the ball to, running backs need to create a target for the quarterback. This is done by placing your inside arm on the top facing one way, and your outside arm on the bottom facing the other way. Both arms should be parallel to the ground. Then the quarterback can stick the ball into your gut. Don't forget to close your arms around the ball and cling to it tightly.

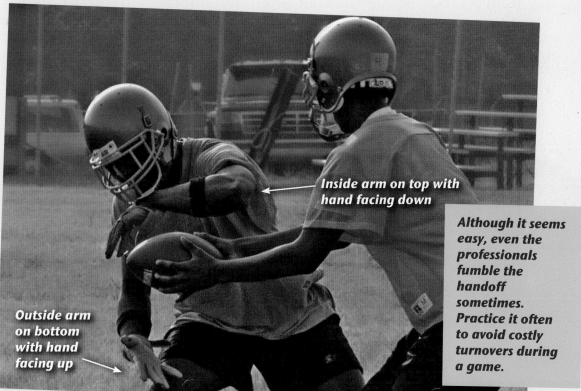

Inside arm on top with hand facing down

Outside arm on bottom with hand facing up

Although it seems easy, even the professionals fumble the handoff sometimes. Practice it often to avoid costly turnovers during a game.

PROTECTING THE BALL

The running back's most important job is to protect the ball. It is best to protect the ball with two hands. However, a running back can move faster holding the ball with one hand (and you can use the other hand to shed would-be tacklers). The best way to do this is to hold the ball high and tight. Hold it around the nose of the football. Squeeze it against your biceps, shoving the other end into your armpit. Keep it just below your shoulder. You can practice protecting the ball by carrying around a medicine ball or a heavier football. This will help you prepare to hold on to a regular football when defenders are trying to rip it away from you.

When you see a "hit" coming, prepare for contact. You can cover the ball with both arms for extra protection. This is especially helpful if there are multiple defenders around you.

PRO TIPS AND TRICKS

In a conversation with fellow great NFL running back Chris Johnson, Minnesota Vikings superstar Adrian Peterson gave him the following advice: "I play the game to be the best player ever to play the game. That's my mentality."

Keep it high and tight against your body.

Stuff the other end into your armpit.

Place hand around the nose of the football

You can use your other hand to fend off tacklers.

Minnesota Vikings running back Adrian Peterson has been selected to the Pro Bowl each of his first four seasons in the NFL. He also holds the single-game rushing record with 296 yards. However, early in his career he had problems with ball security. In his first three NFL seasons, he had twenty fumbles. But after hard work and training in the off-season, Peterson only had one fumble in the 2010 season.

RUNNING TO "DAYLIGHT"

When you see a hole, hit it hard. The "hole" is where the offensive linemen move defenders out of the way in a designed play. While running forward, you may see what is called "daylight." This means you will see an area with no defenders in your path. Run forward, but be prepared to make lateral cuts to avoid defenders. Avoid running backward or sideways because you don't want to lose yards on a running play. When you're not going forward, it gives defenders more time to tackle you.

A good running back should also keep a low center of gravity. This means to keep your pad level low to make it more difficult for bigger players to tackle you. This also helps you drive through players when they hit you. Also, by keeping your legs pumping, you keep your momentum moving forward, even if you're being tackled.

A "stiff arm" can be a great way to break free from would-be tacklers. As a tackler approaches, extend your arm and push the defender away. But don't grab his facemask, or you'll be called for a penalty.

THEN AND NOW

In the early days of the game, football was such a run-oriented game that forward passes were not even allowed until 1905, and then only on a limited basis. Before that, running backs would sometimes lateral, or toss, the ball to a player running alongside or behind them.

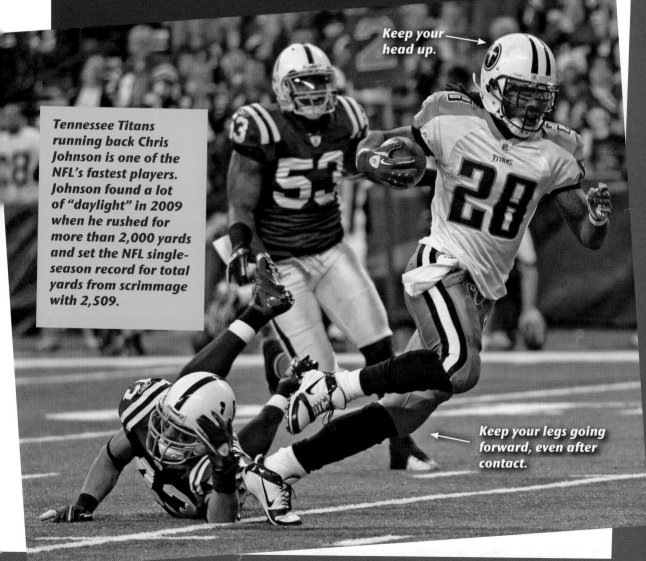

Keep your head up.

Tennessee Titans running back Chris Johnson is one of the NFL's fastest players. Johnson found a lot of "daylight" in 2009 when he rushed for more than 2,000 yards and set the NFL single-season record for total yards from scrimmage with 2,509.

Keep your legs going forward, even after contact.

# RUNNING VISION

Running backs need to have great vision. This means you need to see the field as you run forward with the ball. This will allow you to use your blockers to your advantage. Don't run past the big guys out in front of the play, whose job it is to block defensive players for you. Sometimes, you might have to slow down in order to stay behind your blockers and cut back behind them. Some running backs in the NFL reward their offensive linemen—their blockers—with gifts if they do a good job during the season.

A good running back must be patient. If you run ahead of your blockers or hit the hole too early, you might lose yards. Wait for the play to develop, then explode through the hole. When multiple tacklers converge, protect the ball with two hands.

MORE THAN JUST A RUNNER

A balanced offensive attack blends a good running game with a strong passing game. That means running backs must block for their quarterback during passing plays. Sometimes, it means going out on a passing route to become a receiving target for the quarterback. It's important to learn what is and isn't allowed when blocking. You don't want to get called for a costly holding penalty that will move your team back ten additional yards.

Great running backs must be able to do it all: run, catch, and block. Jim Brown (#32) is one of the greatest running backs in NFL history. One of the most dominating offensive players the NFL has ever had, Brown won three Most Valuable Player awards and was first-team All-Pro in eight consecutive seasons.

DID YOU KNOW?

The NFL used to be a running league with teams rushing the ball much more than passing. NFL great Jim Brown led the NFL in rushing yards for eight out of nine seasons in the 1950s and 1960s. No one has come close to that mark.

LINE PLAY

Have you ever heard a coach or sports announcer say that the game of football is won and lost in the trenches? They are referring to the line of scrimmage, or the spot on the field where the ball is placed. This is where the play starts, where the center snaps the ball to the quarterback.

Most football experts believe whichever team controls the line of scrimmage is the team that will win the game. In other words, if the offensive line is able to open up holes for their running backs and prevent the quarterback from getting sacked, then that team will likely win. On the other hand, if the defensive line is able to fill holes and sack the quarterback, then its chances of winning are better.

The positions along the offensive and defensive lines are not considered glamorous. Not many pro football fans can name a team's starting center or left guard. But every once in a while, linemen get the credit they deserve.

So how do you block? How do you shed a block and make a tackle? Let's find out.

The team that can dominate the line of scrimmage is usually the team that wins the game.

11 RUN BLOCKING

Offensive linemen have a slight advantage over the defense. The offensive line—the center, two guards, and two tackles— know the play and exactly where they will go. They also know what kind of block they will use.

The main type of block used in youth football is called drive blocking. This block, used for running plays, starts with the lineman in a crouch with one hand on the ground. This is called a three-point stance. Then with your head up, looking at your opponent's number, step forward with the same foot as the shoulder you use to hit your opponent. Stay low and continue moving your feet to push the defensive lineman backward.

Keep your hands inside your opponent's shoulders. If you reach outside the pads or hook your arm around him, you risk being called for a holding penalty.

When run blocking, get your body lower than your defender and drive him backward, using your legs to push you forward. This team uses a blocking sled during training. This type of drill helps with run blocking.

12 BLOCKING FOR THE TRAP

Another basic running play that requires a different type of block is a trap play. This type of play means that one of the defensive linemen goes unblocked. He normally runs forward out of the play, creating a nice hole for the running back. But the key to the play is the "pulling" guard. While most of the linemen are moving one way, the guard steps backward and then runs behind his teammates in front of the running back. It is the guard's job to block the first person in his way, or the "trapped" defender, who is now in the backfield.

DID YOU KNOW?

During the 1980s, the offensive line of the Washington Redskins became as famous as the team's star quarterback and running back. They were nicknamed "the Hogs," and they won three Super Bowls. Redskins fans wore pig-snout masks in honor of their beloved hogs.

Whether you're blocking for a trap, draw, sweep, or any other type of running play, the goal is to create a hole for the running back to go through.

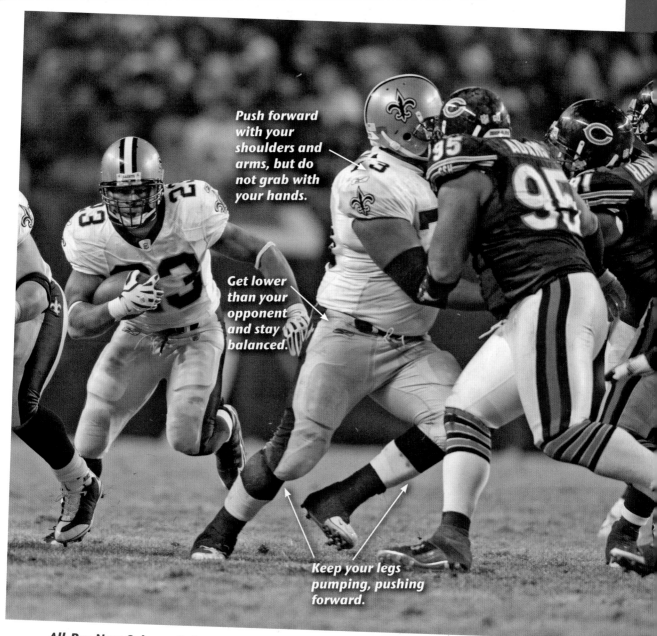

Push forward with your shoulders and arms, but do not grab with your hands.

Get lower than your opponent and stay balanced.

Keep your legs pumping, pushing forward.

All-Pro New Orleans Saints guard Jahri Evans (right, white jersey) helps open up a hole for running back Pierre Thomas (left) during a game against the Chicago Bears. Footwork and balance are very important parts of run blocking. In addition to driving defenders backward during a rushing play, offensive linemen also need to be agile enough to block for runs toward the outside of the field.

 # PASS BLOCKING

When your quarterback calls a pass play, the offensive line will have to use a different type of block. The goal of pass blocking is not to drive your defender back. Instead, it is to keep the other team from sacking your quarterback. The idea is to give your passer enough time to throw the ball to an open receiver.

Starting again in a three-point stance, blockers stand up quickly in a crouch once the ball is snapped. Hands and arms should be outstretched in front of you. Keep your feet moving so you can switch directions quickly depending on how the defensive player is charging at you. While you use your shoulders during a run block, in pass blocking, you use your hands to keep pushing your opponent off you. You still want to push him back, away from your quarterback. Be careful not to grab or you might get called for a holding penalty.

PRO TIPS AND TRICKS

After a big win against the Pittsburgh Steelers, New England Patriots quarterback Tom Brady gave all the credit to his blockers—his offensive line. He said it was very important that they had played together as a unit for a long time. "I love these guys," he said. "Those are my boys. I'm proud of the way they compete and fight every day. It's a great group."

Eyes on the defender

Hips stay in front of the defender, your weight slightly forward

Arms extended to push the defender back

Stay on the balls of your feet, pushing forward when you make contact with the defender.

Michael Oher plays the all-important position of left tackle, which protects the right-handed quarterback's "blind side." Oher's story has been told in a book and movie called **The Blind Side.**

14 DEFENSIVE LINE

Defensive linemen—whether they are defensive tackles, defensive ends, or nose tackles—have to be agile, quick, and strong enough to shed blocks. Defensive linemen can line up in a three-point stance. They can line up in a four-point stance with two hands down, or even in an upright stance with no hands on the ground.

On the defensive line, you need to remain balanced. You will be blocked easily if you play out of control and off balance. Keep your feet shoulder width apart. Stay low as you work to get rid of the blockers and tackle the player with the ball. As a defensive lineman, you must react quickly to the play in front of you. You will have to recognize whether it is a running play, a passing play, a trap, a reverse, or something else. Even if you are not able to make a tackle or pressure the quarterback, you can still disrupt a play by occupying blockers and filling a hole. This frees up the linebackers so they can make the tackle.

A defensive lineman's job is to take on blockers. Always engage the player in front of you. Then work to get around the blocker and pursue, or chase, the ball carrier or quarterback.

15 PATIENCE ON DEFENSE

Perhaps the toughest part of playing on the defensive line is to have patience. The natural instinct is to race forward as quick as you can and hit the quarterback. But traps, screen passes, counters, and other types of plays take advantage of the defensive lineman's aggressiveness. So, your first responsibility is to hit the man in front of you, engage him, and then look for the ball. Finally, if the ball pops loose, defensive linemen should fall on the ball and pull it close to their bodies. You should not try to pick up the ball and run with it.

One of the most important jobs for defensive linemen, especially defensive ends, is rushing the passer. Chicago Bears defensive end Julius Peppers is a dominant pass rusher, and he uses various techniques to get to the quarterback. You can try the speed rush, which is to sprint around your opponent to sack the quarterback. The "bull rush" is to use your strength and push the offensive lineman backward into the quarterback.

THEN AND NOW

Defensive linemen used to be able to swing their arms and slap the helmets of offensive linemen in front of them. But the NFL made the "head slap" illegal, calling it the "Deacon Jones rule." It was named after Deacon Jones, the Hall of Fame defensive end that perfected the move.

DEFENSE AND SPECIAL TEAMS

How many times have you watched or played in a football game that came down to a field goal try? Or how about that key interception? Good defense and special teams are key parts for any winning football team.

Special teams are the players on the field during any sort of kicking play. This includes kickoffs, punts, field-goal attempts, and extra points. Every football drive that ends in a kick is a good one. Even punting the ball away is better than a turnover.

The defense is made up of the defensive line, linebackers, and defensive backs. Many times, defense and special teams are overlooked in youth football. Here are some tips to make you better.

 HOW TO TACKLE

The ball carrier is coming your way. If he gets past you, the other team scores a touchdown. You need to tackle the player with the ball. But what is the correct way? The idea behind a proper tackle is to throw yourself through the ball carrier. Build up enough speed to stop the guy with ball.

Keep your knees bent and hips low before any contact is made. When you are close enough, push off your feet and drive through the ball carrier. Hit the ball carrier with your shoulder pads. Then wrap your arms around the ball carrier under his butt or thighs to throw him off balance. Now, it's important that you get your head out across the player's body, blocking his path. But do not lead with your helmet. This was big news during the 2010 NFL season. The league cracked down on helmet-to-helmet hits that can cause serious injury.

San Francisco 49ers linebacker Patrick Willis tackles Carolina Panthers running back DeAngelo Williams. Willis has led the NFL in tackles twice in his career. Tackling requires speed, strength, and smarts. Don't slow down when you get to the ball carrier. Drive through the ball carrier and wrap him up around his waist or legs. Don't try to tackle someone by the upper body, because it is easier for him to break away from you.

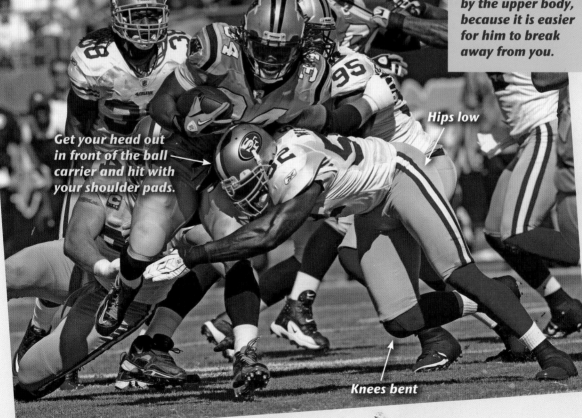

Get your head out in front of the ball carrier and hit with your shoulder pads.

Hips low

Knees bent

There are usually three to four linebackers on the field. They line up about three to four yards behind the defensive line. While the line players have one hand on the ground in a three-point stance, the linebackers stand up. Depending on where they are playing—in the middle or on the outside—their jobs are different. The middle linebacker, or inside linebackers, normally "spy" on the quarterback and react to his movement. If the quarterback drops back to pass the ball, these linebackers will often drop back into pass coverage to help cover the receivers. Outside linebackers will often rush on the outside to sack the quarterback or at least force him to move up out of the pocket, or comfort zone.

Of course, linebackers are also key players in stopping the other team's rushing attack. They must charge up and fill the holes in the line of scrimmage when they recognize a running play. Many times the linebackers will have "keys," or certain players they watch, to tell them if the play is a run or a pass.

There are times where your coach might call a "blitz" on defense. During this play, additional defenders rush the quarterback to get a sack quickly. Linebackers are often used to blitz the quarterback. In this photo, Green Bay Packers linebacker Clay Matthews sacks quarterback Jay Cutler during a regular season game.

Good linebackers must be able to play against running and passing plays. Depending on the type of play, a linebacker might need to drop into pass coverage, rush the quarterback, or tackle the ball carrier. Good defensive teams rally around the ball, which means wherever the ball goes, the defenders are there, quickly in pursuit.

# 18 PASS COVERAGE

The defensive backs are the defense's last line against the offense's passing attack. Defensive backs are typically two cornerbacks and two safeties. The safeties play in the middle of the field and the corners play on the outside. Many people say that defensive backs have the toughest job on the football field. They have to be great athletes, with terrific speed and quickness, and they cannot be afraid to make a tough tackle. While defensive backs need to rush the line of scrimmage and make tackles during running plays, their main job is to defend the pass. The two main types of coverage are man-to-man and zone.

In man-to-man coverage, the defensive back is assigned a player. He has to follow that player and prevent him from catching a pass. In zone coverage, the players defend a certain area on the field and defend passes thrown in that area.

A great skill that defensive backs need is backpedaling. Defensive backs usually spend a lot of time at practice working on their backpedaling skills. They also need to work on agility and leaping ability.

THEN AND NOW

In 1869, when American football was invented, a touchdown was worth two points and a field goal was worth five points. Of course, in today's game, a touchdown is worth six points and a field goal is worth only three.

New York Jets All-Pro cornerback Darrelle Revis (left) is nicknamed "Revis Island" for his ability to shut down the opposing team's best receiver. Cornerbacks have a difficult job in pass coverage. They cannot always see the quarterback release the ball because they need to stay locked on to the receiver. A good tip to know when the ball is coming is to watch the receiver's eyes and hands. When he puts his hands up to catch it or turns his head to find the ball, that's when you get ready to deflect it away.

19 PUNTING AND SPECIAL TEAMS COVERAGE

As the punter, you line up about seven to ten yards behind the center or long snapper. Stand with your feet shoulder-width apart. Cock your arms at the elbows so your hands are out in front of you. Your kicking foot should be slightly behind your non-kicking foot. Never take your eyes off the ball as it soars toward you. Watch the ball as it lands in your hands all the way until you punt it. Turn the ball so that the laces are facing up. Then step forward with your kicking foot and a small step with your non-kicking foot as you drop the ball. Then kick it!

Kickoff and punt coverage is also essential. After your teammate punts the ball to the other team, what should you do? The first thing is to avoid any blockers in your way. Second, stay in your lane as you run down the field. Third, make the tackle. There is nothing worse than seeing your punt or kickoff returned for a touchdown.

A good tip is to never leave your feet. Diving or leaping can be dangerous, and it leaves your spot on the field unprotected. A good drill to practice is called punting chaos. The punt and punt-receiving teams are on the field. The punter makes his kick but only the players right of the snapper are allowed to run down the field and cover the punt. The same thing with the return team. Then do it again with the left side of both teams.

DID YOU KNOW?

One of the rarest plays in pro football is called the quick kick. This is when the quarterback punts the ball on a down when the other team is not expecting it. This is done to trap the other team into bad field position because they will not have a returner set up to receive the punt.

Punting is an important part of the field position battle in football. Punting is more about technique than strength. You need to be able to punt it a long distance but also with accuracy. Sometimes, it's more important where you kick the ball than how far you kick it. Often, it's important to punt the ball high as well. Good hang time allows the punt coverage to get downfield to tackle the punt returner.

20 KICKING FIELD GOALS

Few plays in football can be as nerve-wracking as a field goal try. So many things have to go perfectly. First, the long snapper, with one hand below the ball and one hand on top, must snap the ball back using his wrists so that it is a tight spiral.

The holder must hold his front hand out and the back hand on the kicking tee. He must catch the ball and place it on the tee with the laces facing away from the kicker. Then he uses an index finger to hold the ball down.

The kicker, who started with his feet apart, now takes two steps and kicks the ball, making sure to keep his head down the entire time. Kick the ball with your instep, the bottom of the laces on your shoe.

Plant the non-kicking foot next to the ball, aimed at your target.

Holder keeps the ball in place with index finger.

Strike through the ball with your instep, or the bottom of your laces.

A field goal attempt requires a good snap, a good hold, and a good kick. There is a proper technique to each one.

Kickers have to stay calm in pressure situations. All-Pro kicker Adam Vinatieri has been a clutch kicker his whole career, including kicking game-winning field goals in two Super Bowls.

PRO TIPS AND TRICKS

One of the best clutch kickers in the NFL, Adam Vinatieri, says no matter how great you have played or how many games you have won with great kicks, the only one that matters is the next kick you make. "Every time you step out on the field you have to redo it. Just because you've done it in the past doesn't mean anything."

FUN TRICKS AND TRAINING

To succeed in football, players need to be in great shape and train nearly year-round.

In the NFL, for example, teams start holding training sessions in March, followed by official training camp in July. Exhibition games begin in August and the full slate of games goes from September through January.

For younger players, like those in youth football, it is very important to plan out a training schedule with your parents, coaches, and doctor. Never start an exercise program without going to the doctor first. Also, weight lifting is not for everyone. Make sure you get an exercise program that is right for you.

 AGILITY DRILLS

What's the best way to train? There are several methods. However, the best way to strengthen the muscles and build the endurance needed to play football is by actually playing the game. Scrimmages, or practice games, can help you gauge what you need to work on. During a football game, you will be called on to use a lot of reserve energy. You can't just sit down and rest when you want to. Your teammates depend on you.

Many coaches use something called the Dot Drill to help players improve their quickness, agility, and endurance. The drill is simple and resembles the childhood game of hopscotch. Start with your feet spread apart. Then jump and land on a painted spot (or put down some sort of marker) about a yard in front of you so that your feet have now come together. Then jump forward again on two markers or dots that are a yard in front of you and spread apart. This should be similar in distance to your starting point. Then do it backward. Time yourself and see how many you can do in a minute.

Agility drills are a great way to improve a player's quickness and acceleration. Seattle Seahawks players take part in an agility drill during mini-camp. These types of drills will also improve your endurance.

DID YOU KNOW?

Former guard Larry Allen of the Dallas Cowboys is regarded as the strongest man in NFL history. He twice defended his ESPN "Strongest Man in the NFL" title and is said to have bench-pressed seven hundred pounds!

22 CONDITIONING

Here are a few common conditioning drills. Using cones, mark off an area of forty square yards. Basically, this is a series of forty-yard sprints, with a twist. The first forty yards of the square should be done with a player backpedaling. This resembles what a defensive back might do. When you turn the corner, the next sprint can be the karaoke drill—a sideways run with your legs crossing in front of and then behind the other. The next sprint can be a sideways shuffle where the legs do not cross at all. The final one can be an all-out sprint. This drill helps increase speed, endurance, and agility.

A fun drill for quarterbacks and receivers is simple, too. Have three or four receivers stand at the line of scrimmage and assign each one of them a number. The center snaps the ball to the quarterback, who drops back to pass. The coach then calls out a random number and the quarterback must pass it to the receiver assigned with that number. When you've mastered that drill, add some defensive backs to make it more difficult.

A similar type drill can involve offensive and defensive linemen formed in a circle. The coach throws a loose ball into the center of the circle and calls out two numbers. The players assigned with those numbers run into the circle and try to recover the fumble before the other player does.

THEN AND NOW

In football's early days, players wore leather helmets. Now, the players have become so much faster and stronger that the NFL continues to develop safer helmets to keep its players from getting hurt during contact.

23 TERRIBLE 20s

Most football players hate the "Terrible 20s" because it is a long, tiring drill. But this tough drill will help tone and condition your entire body.

Split the team into two groups and place them on opposite goal lines. When the coach blows his whistle, one group will do twenty push-ups while the other group does twenty sit-ups. Then they sprint the length of the field. The group that did the push-ups first now does nineteen sit-ups and vice versa. The drill is complete when the numbers reach zero. It's a tiring drill, but the results will be obvious on game day.

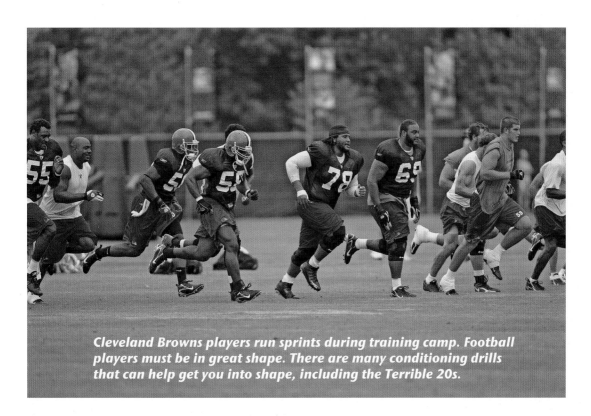

Cleveland Browns players run sprints during training camp. Football players must be in great shape. There are many conditioning drills that can help get you into shape, including the Terrible 20s.

24 TWO-HAND TOUCH

What about practicing football just for fun? A fun game to play after school with your friends is two-hand-touch football. You don't need any protective equipment.

Split up into even teams, usually five or six to a side. You play a normal football game, except a tackle is made by landing two hands at the same time on the player with the ball. Usually, the defense keeps one player on the line of scrimmage to rush the quarterback after counting to a certain number of seconds. The game is complete with punts, kickoffs, and a time limit.

There are schoolyard football games you can play that don't require equipment, such as two-hand-touch football. Flag football is another fun, noncontact game that's great for practicing your football skills.

PRO TIPS AND TRICKS

Pro Bowl quarterback Donovan McNabb likes to have what he calls a "hell week" of training every year the week before official team training camp begins. Held near his Arizona home, McNabb invites his teammates—usually running backs and wide receivers—to join him. The workouts begin early in the morning and go all day. McNabb says it's a great way for new teammates to bond.

25 FUN PLAYS

Teams will occasionally try a trick play that is meant to totally fool the other team. These plays are a lot of fun to watch and even more fun to attempt yourself.

One play is called the "flea flicker." In this play, the quarterback pitches or hands the ball off to a running back. The running back takes a step or two forward as if he is going to run the ball. But the running back turns quickly and tosses the ball back to the quarterback, who then throws a pass downfield to a receiver.

Sometimes, teams will also fake a punt or field goal and run or pass the ball out of the kicking formation.

Many times at the end of a close game, you will see a play known as the "Hail Mary." This "prayer" involves sending three or four receivers to one corner of the end zone. The quarterback then heaves the ball toward that area with the hope that a tipped ball will end up in the arms of his wide receiver.

Trick plays can surprise the opposing team's defense. Plus, they are fun to practice. You might find yourself breaking away from the defense to score the game-winning touchdown!

GLOSSARY

backpedal—To run backward, taking short, quick steps.

center—The position between the two guards on the offensive line. This player hikes or snaps the ball to the quarterback.

drop back—The quarterback takes the snap from the center and moves back between three and seven steps from the line of scrimmage on passing plays.

extra point—The kick attempt taken after a touchdown is scored. It is worth one point.

facemask—The plastic part of the football helmet that protects the player's face.

line of scrimmage—This is the spot on the football field where the ball is placed and where the play begins. Offensive linemen set up on the line of scrimmage.

momentum—The force or speed of movement.

penalty—When a player or team does something on the field that is not allowed. Examples of penalties include holding, illegal motion, offsides, pass interference, unnecessary roughness, and delay of game, among others.

pocket—The throwing area behind the offensive line, usually between the hash marks on the field, where the quarterback looks to find a receiver.

punt—This usually occurs on fourth down, when a team elects to kick the ball to the other team.

route—The path a receiver, tight end, or running back is expected to run during a passing play.

screen pass—A tricky pass play that is meant to fool the defensive team into rushing after the quarterback before the quarterback throws a short pass to a receiver or running back behind the line of scrimmage.

FURTHER READING

Books

Buckley, Jr., James. *Scholastic Ultimate Guide to Football.* New York: Franklin Watts, 2010.

Doeden, Matt. *Play Football Like a Pro: Key Skills and Tips.* Mankato, Minn.: Capstone Press, 2011.

Jacobs, Greg. *The Everything Kids' Football Book.* Avon, Mass.: Adams Media, 2008.

Madden, John, and Bill Gutman. *John Madden's Heroes of Football: The Story of America's Game.* New York: Dutton Children's Books, 2006.

Stewart, Mike, and Mike Kennedy. *Touchdown: The Power and Precision of Football's Perfect Play.* Minneapolis, Minn.: Millbrook Press, 2010.

Thomas, Keltie. *How Football Works.* Toronto: Maple Tree Press, 2010.

Internet Addresses

Howcast.com: Football Skills Videos
<http://www.howcast.com/categories/1385-Football-Skills>

NFLRush: The National Football League Kids' Web Site
<http://www.nflrush.com/>

WePlay.com: Youth Football Drills & Skills
<http://www.weplay.com/youth-football/drills>

INDEX

A

Allen, Larry, 41

B

Blanda, George, 8
blocking
    drive (run), 23–25
    holding penalty,
       21, 23, 26
    pass, 26–27
    trap play, 24
Brady, Tom, 26
Brown, Jim, 21

C

center of gravity, 18

D

"daylight," 18, 19
Deacon Jones rule, 29
defense, 28–35
defensive backs,
    34–35

F

field goals, 34, 38–39
flea flicker play, 45

G

gripping a football, 6

H

Hail Mary play, 45
hand-off exchange,
    14–15
head slap, 29
history of football, 12,
    19, 21, 29, 34, 42

J

Johnson, Chris, 16

L

linebackers, 28,
    32–33
linemen, 22–29, 42
line of scrimmage, 8,
    22, 32, 34

M

Manning, Peyton, 6
McNabb, Donovan,
    44

P

passing
    ball protection, 16
    footwork, 7
    gripping a football,
       6
    overview, 5
    throwing form, 10
    throwing stance,
       8–9
Peterson, Adrian, 16
pulling guard, 24
punting, 36–37

Q

quarterbacks, 5–10,
    14, 15, 42
quick kick, 37

R

receiving, 11–13
running backs, 14–21

rushing
    exchange, 15
    overview, 14
    protecting the ball,
       16–17, 20
    running style,
       18–19
    vision, 20

S

special teams, 30,
    36–39
stiff arm, 18

T

tackling, 30–31
three-point stance,
    23, 26, 28, 32
tight end position, 12
touchdowns, 34
training
    agility, 40–41
    ball protection, 16
    conditioning, 42
    preparation, 6
    punting chaos, 36
    Terrible 20s, 43
trap play, 24
two-hand-touch, 44

V

Vinatieri, Adam, 39